WARM-UP EXERCISES
FOR GUITAR

By John Stix And Yoichi Arakawa

ISBN 0-7935-6645-2

HAL•LEONARD®
CORPORATION
7777 W. BLUEMOUND RD. P.O. BOX 13819 MILWAUKEE, WI 53213

INTRODUCTION

Playing the guitar is probably no less violent than playing football. Both demand talent, skill, strength, speed, agility and contact. And in order to play, once the music or the ball is in motion, all hands have to work together to make it happen. There is pushing and hitting, abrupt stops, and lightning fast changes of direction. Neither is something you can do well if you're not in shape for it. And one of the worst things you can do in either case is play full-on without warming up. Do that and you're bound to get hurt. Maybe not today, but somewhere down the road, playing could become painful and ultimately harmful.

To educate us on how the pros get ready before hitting the stage, we asked 11 guitarists about their warm-up routines. But to get the ball rolling—or, rather, the blood pumping—the authors offer the following observations when working with any of the exercises in the book:

We found that usually a warm-up or any finger exercise is born out of a player's effort or frustration to overcome a particular passage of a song or a difficult lick. He might invent an exercise that would help or facilitate his technique or the dexterity necessary to play those difficult parts. That's what any exercise or practice should be. It should always be related to and in consideration of the music you are trying to play. Once you get an idea from the guitarists here, invent your own warm-up exercises suitable for your own needs and the type of music you are playing.

On a nuts-and-bolts level, while Eddie Van Halen can call upon his drummer brother Alex when he needs a groove to move, the rest of us will probably call upon the trusty drum machine or a metronome. Tony MacAlpine discussed the importance of playing with a drum machine, saying, "When you practice with a drum machine or metronome, you can lock into the rhythm. It's very easy to make rhythmic mistakes. If you don't have a good understanding of what rhythmic influences are like, you'll get lost with a drum machine. With a drum machine you can fall on the beat, lay back in the groove, or be in front of the beat. The metronome is stiff. It's hard to screw that up. The metronome is a stern teacher."

A universal rule is to always start your warm-ups slowly and increase the tempo gradually. Strive for a smooth, clear, and strong execution of the exercise. Avoid sloppiness, rushing, or dragging. Keep in mind that these ideas are not only good for warm-ups, but excellent for strengthening your fingers as well.

Once you learn an exercise, look away from the music so that you can better concentrate on your own playing.

EXPLAINING TABLATURE

Tablature is a paint-by-number language telling you which notes to play on the fingerboard. Each of the six lines represents a string on the guitar. The numbers in the line indicate which frets to press down. Note that tablature does not indicate the rhythm.

1st string	E
2nd string	B
3rd string	G
4th string	D
5th string	A
6th string	E

NOTATION LEGEND

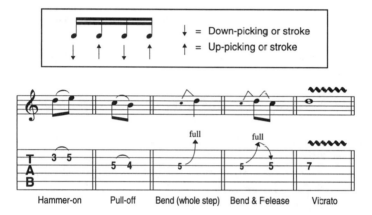

↓ = Down-picking or stroke
↑ = Up-picking or stroke

Hammer-on   Pull-off   Bend (whole step)   Bend & Release   Vibrato

Hammer-on:
Pick the first (lower) note, then "hammer-on" to sound the higher note with another finger by fretting it without picking.

Pull-off:
Place both fingers on the notes to be sounded. Pick the first (higher) note, then sound the lower note by "pulling-off" the finger on the higher note while keeping the lower note fretted.

Bend (whole step):
Pick the note and bend up a whole step (two frets).

Bend & Release:
Pick the note and bend up a whole step, then release the bend back to the original note. All three notes are tied together; only the first note is attacked.

Vibrato:
Vibrate the note by rapidly bending and releasing the string using a left-hand finger, wrist or forearm.

Finger Number:
A number put next to each note.

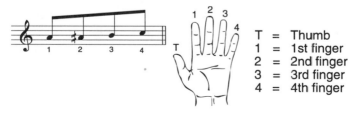

T	= Thumb
1	= 1st finger
2	= 2nd finger
3	= 3rd finger
4	= 4th finger

"I try to impress upon people, and the younger guys especially, to get in the habit of making stretching a part of your daily routine. Tendonitis is not something that you want to deal with. It's a reality. If you are really serious and you play a lot, you practice a lot, or both, it's something that can very easily happen to anyone. I know a lot of people that have played for a long time, and they are struggling with this. It can really alter your life.

"Stretch your shoulder first, because you want to start up there. The idea is you want to warm up and loosen up the muscles before playing. And then you'll want to cool down the tendons and muscles after you get done playing.

"Now, take one arm and cross it over the other. Then take the arm facing your face and gently pull it toward you so it's stretched. You can feel it pull up into your shoulder. Do this for about 20 seconds.

"After the shoulder, I start massaging my forearm. My tendonitis is in the crook of my wrist, from the outer part of the palm, beneath the little finger. There is a tendon right there and it's inflamed all the time. I'll spend time to loosen up this area. Put your hands up, with your elbows out, just beyond your shoulders. Put your hands together so it looks like you are praying. Now slightly lift your elbows and you can feel the stretch.

"Another stretch is to have your palms face away from you. Now take one hand and place it on the other. Palm to palm, one hand is facing away from you, and the other hand is facing you. Have the hand facing you push back slightly on the hand facing away from you. Think of your fingers as one. What you are doing is getting down the forearm.

"The last thing I do is individual fingers. These are very gentle stretches. One hand presses against the other (to look like you are praying), but the fingers are separated. Press one hand against the other. Your fingers go backwards.

"Ideally, if I'm working a lot, I'll try to get going for 15 to 20 minutes first. If I'm having problems and need the full-blown affair, I'll use a moist heat first. I'll put a heating pad with moist heat on the muscles, and then start doing the stretches. Then I play for what seems like forever. At the end, when I'm done playing, I'll ice down. Especially where the prominent areas are. Ideally, the best thing to do is have a sink with ice water in it, and put your whole arm down in it, like a baseball pitcher. It's like sports medicine.

"I urge people to do this because tendonitis is debilitating."

There are things that twist my tendons up that I practice over and over again. It kills me that someone like Steve Vai would say, 'You mean that lick you did?' and just knock it out.
—Joe Satriani*

*Courtesy of *Guitar for the Practicing Musician Magazine*

4

TWO-FINGER EXERCISES
with STEVE VAI

"Did you ever do those exercises where you take your 1st and 2nd finger and you go across the strings? Do that with your 1st and 2nd finger all the way up and down the neck in half steps at four different metronome speeds. Then do that with your 1st and 3rd fingers. Then do it with your 1st and 4th fingers. Then do it with your 2nd and 3rd fingers, all the way up and all the way down. Then your 2nd and 4th fingers, and then your 3rd and 4th fingers. It's a great exercise, because the 3rd and 4th fingers aren't as strong as your 1st and 2nd. Then you do it with skipping a fret. It's the same concept. You do your 1st and 3rd fingers and skip a fret, so you've got two frets between them. Try and do that with your 2nd and 3rd fingers, skipping a fret. And you have to do it just as clean as the 1st and 2nd fingers. If you can do it, believe me, your chops will be 100% improved.

"The metronome speed is up to the user. You have to start really slow so you don't even make one little mistake. I don't do these anymore. God, if I had time to sit and do exercises, that would be great. When I used to do them, I used a metronome because that's all I had."

Ex. 1 is an exercise for finger combinations 1-2, 2-3 and 3-4.

Ex. 1

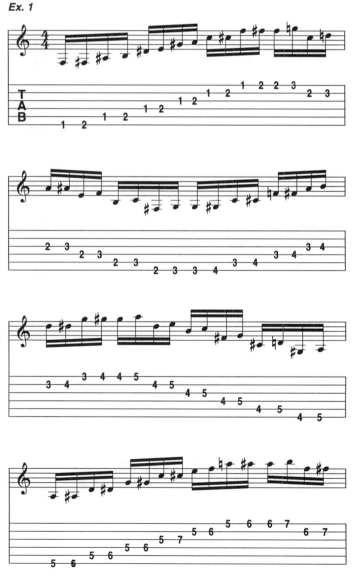

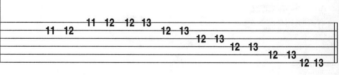

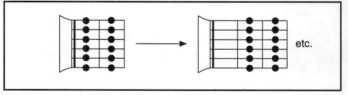

Diagram 1

Ex. 2 is an exercise for finger combinations 1-3, 2-4, and stretching for 1-2, 2-3 and 3-4.

Ex. 2

etc.

Diagram 2

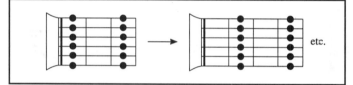

etc.

Ex. 3 is an exercise for finger combinations 1-4 and stretching for 1-3 and 2-4.

Ex. 3

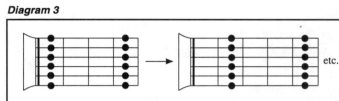

etc.

Diagram 3

etc.

Ex. 4 is an exercise for a finger combination with stretching 1-4.

Ex. 4

etc.

Diagram 4

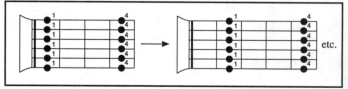

etc.

BASIC THREE- AND FOUR-FINGER EXERCISES
with ROBIN TROWER

"Many years ago Robert Fripp gave me a very good warm-up exercise which I used to use. He had me use all of my fingers, starting at the bottom string, first fret. You play a note on every fret. So you go 1, 2, 3, 4 on the bottom string, and then you go up on each string from low E to high E. So you go on the E string for four frets, A string four frets and so on. After you've played the last note (G#) with your pinkie on the high E string, move up a fret and come back down the strings 4, 3, 2, 1.

"You are going up four frets, then moving up one fret, and coming back down. You start by using all of your fingers. Then what he had me do was drop one out. So you start 1, 3, 4 all the way up, move up one, and come back 4, 3, 1. Then you just do a combination of any two fingers. It was a very good exercise; no doubt about it. It gets your finger coordination going. I haven't done that one in a while, but I did do it quite religiously the year he gave it to me. He is a very good teacher."

Ex. 5 is the most basic four-finger exercise, which is good for developing equal strength in each finger.

Ex. 5

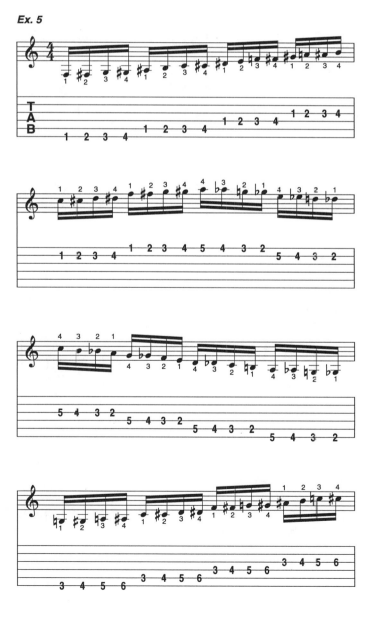

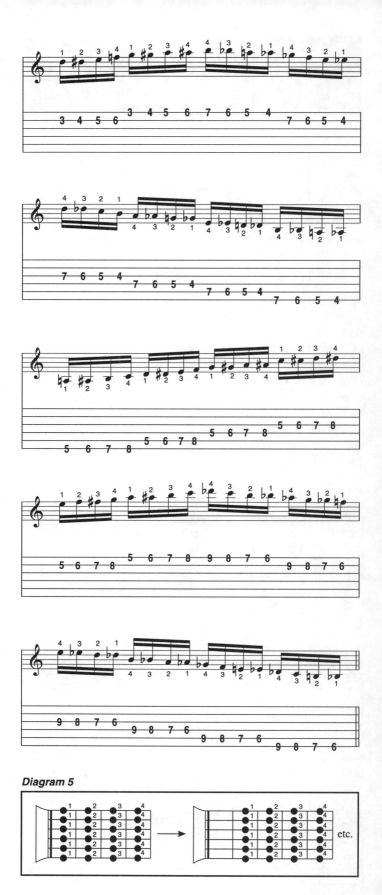

Diagram 5

Ex. 6 shows one of the three-finger exercises. See below for other possible combinations.

1-2-3, 1-3-2, 2-1-3, 1-2-4, 1-4-2, 2-1-4, 1-3-4, 1-4-3, 3-1-4
2-3-4, 2-4-3, 3-2-4, 3-2-1, 2-3-1, 3-1-2, 4-2-1, 2-4-1, 4-1-2
4-3-1, 3-4-1, 4-1-3, 4-3-2, 3-4-2, 4-2-3

Picking on triplets: 1. down-down-down
2. down-up-down, down-up-down
3. down-up-down, up-down-up

Picking on triplets

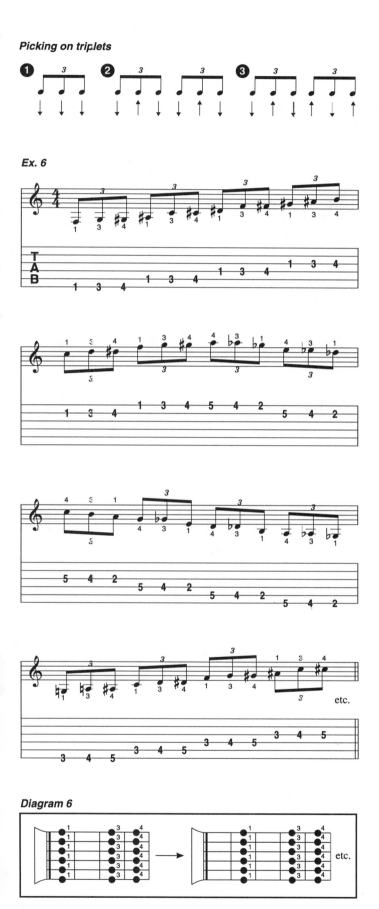

Ex. 6

Diagram 6

RANDOM THREE-FINGER EXERCISES AND SKIPPING STRINGS

with MARTY FRIEDMAN

"What I do is something that Jason (Becker) showed me. It's not really an exercise, and I made it a lot simpler than what he does. Use any two strings; I take the E and A string. But you can use anything that moves the fingers very, very slowly. No need to play warm-up exercises fast. What's the point? Usually, I don't have time to do anything. I just get handed the guitar and go out and play. I try and go over the first solo before I hit the stage. If I play the first solo, then it's kind of in my head a little bit. The adrenaline rush doesn't kill me. Sometimes the adrenaline is so out there at the beginning of our set that I can barely play the first solo without thinking. If it's in my head a little bit, I can go on autopilot.

"This exercise should be played all over the place, in scale, out of scale, stretched out. Just limber up."

Ex. 7 is the combination Marty described, going up the neck. Don't forget to do the same coming back down the neck as well.

Ex. 7

Diagram 7

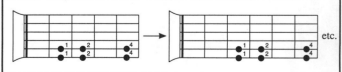

etc.

Marty's exercise is a combination of 2-4-1 and 4-1-2, which are two possibilities of the many three-finger combinations that we saw in Robin Trower's exercise.

Ex. 8 is the combination going across the neck. You can go up the neck as far as you want.

Ex. 8

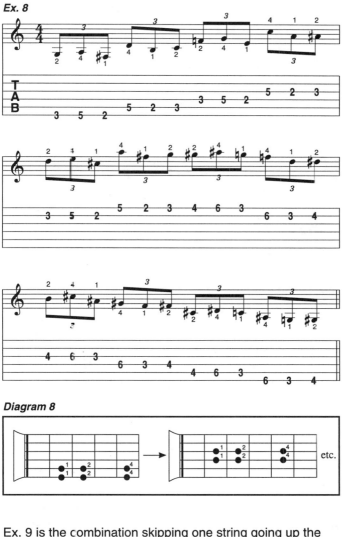

Diagram 8

Ex. 9 is the combination skipping one string going up the neck.

Ex. 9

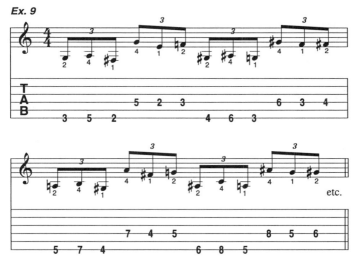

Diagram 9

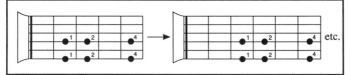

Ex. 10 is the combination skipping a string across the neck. Now experiment with other combinations of your choice in the same manner.

Ex. 10

Diagram 10

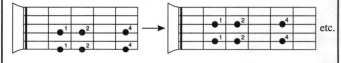

I warm up before I go on stage, but the best way to warm up for me is playing. We have a small drum kit in the dressing room, and our drummer, Mike Mangini, the king of warming up, does the sickest warm-up things. I just jam along with him. I think the best thing to do is use common sense. You start off nice and slow, whether it's a pentatonic thing or anything you choose. Play with a slow pace for a while and then sort of build it up. At the end of my warm up, Mike and I are out of control. We're playing way too many notes. But, if you warm up, you feel much better when you go on stage.

—Nuno Bettencourt

THREE-FINGER EXERCISES USING ARPEGGIOS
with PETER FRAMPTON

"I got most of my warm-up exercises from Steve Morse. I start on the A note of the low E string and play these arpeggios, moving a half step up the neck after each pattern. Sometimes I start on G. I go all the way up to the 12th fret. I do that as part of a few warm-ups that I do in the dressing room before I go on. It's good for the left hand. But do it for both hands, really, because you are using up and down strokes. It's just one of a few that I do that hopefully gets my coordination going and it also reminds my little finger to play."

Ex.11 is the Dom 9 arpeggio that Peter Frampton warms up with. After you get to the 12th fret, don't forget to come back down.

Ex. 11

Diagram 11

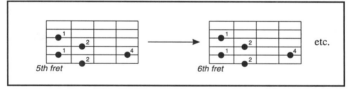

CHROMATIC SCALES AND PICKING EXERCISES
with WARREN DeMARTINI

"When I warm up, it's pretty simple. I just work on playing all down-strokes for a while, and then all up-strokes for a while, gradually mixing in to down and up. The whole thing takes about a half an hour. I'll do it till I can feel it, and then I stop and shake out. I play a chromatic scale starting with my index finger on the A note of the E string, and go chromatically up from there. Instead of going up to C♯ on the E, I go down to C♯ on the A string. So your hand only moves one fret. You play C♯ and D on the A string with the index finger and continue on with the rest of your fingers till you play F with the pinkie. Move down one fret and one string to the F♯, on the D string. Play that and G with the index finger and go up three frets with the next three fingers. Continue this pattern on the G string. When you get to the B string you go down one string, without moving back one fret. The index finger plays the E, and the pattern continues for four notes. For the high E string you go down one fret and one string to the G♯, on the E string. Play G♯, and A with the index finger and then finish the pattern all the way up to the C with your pinkie. I'll play around with this idea. Sometimes I'll do that exercises chromatically up and down the neck a couple of times at different speeds. For me, warming up is getting the left and right hand aligned. I learned that exercise from a friend of mine, Ron Wolfson. It's a good way to get moving. I blend downstrokes, up-strokes and combinations of the two. I found getting that loose was a good thing to do."

Ex.12 shows the chromatic scale from the low A to high C♯ across the neck.

Picking: 1. All down-strokes
2. All up-strokes
3. Alternate picking

Ex. 12

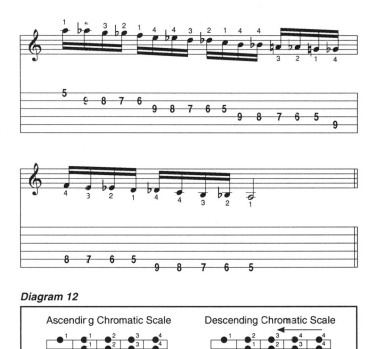

Diagram 12

Ascending Chromatic Scale   Descending Chromatic Scale

4th fret   5th fret

I don't usually just sit down and practice scales. I think that is the most boring thing. It's like eating a sprout sandwich. Not for me; I need a different kind of meat. I play to records a lot. I play along with John Coltrane's 'Naima' and 'My Favorite Things,' and try to hang in there with McCoy (Tyner) and Elvin (Jones). Once the record is over, that's a good warmup exercise.

You can't play what Trane plays, so all you can do is just play the melody like he does and then just try to hang in there. When you see a hole, try to fill it like Walter Payton. When you see an opening, penetrate. That's about it. Most of the time I just put my guitar down after about 15 or 20 minutes, because when Trane and Elvin Jones take off, nobody can hang in there. Just do your best. That's the best exercise I can think of. A daily dose of Trane is the exercise that everybody should have.

—Carlos Santana

WHOLE-TONE SCALES
with ROBBIE KRIEGER

"I will just do some scales, whole-tones, half-tones and altered scales. I'll work on a particular song that I might be having trouble with."

A whole-tone scale is a six-note scale made up entirely of whole steps. So there will be one fret between every note in the scale. Which means there are no chromatics or half steps in this scale. There are only two whole-tone scales. The second whole-note scale starts one fret away from the first one and uses the six notes which were not used in the first whole-tone scale. Having no specific key center, any note on the scale can act as a root note.

Ex. 13 is a G whole-tone scale in 2nd position: G, A, B, C♯ (D♭), D♯ (E♭), F. Watch for the stretch with the 4th finger.

Ex. 13

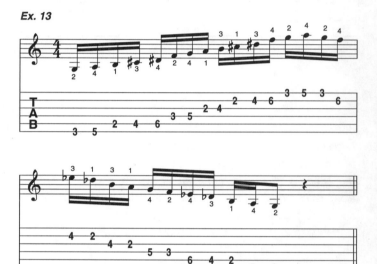

Diagram 13

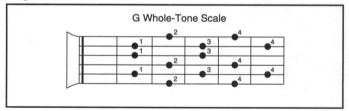

Ex. 14 is a G♯ whole-tone scale in 4th position: G♯ (A♭), A♯ (B♭), C, D, E, F♯ (G♭). Watch for the stretch with the 1st finger.

Ex. 14

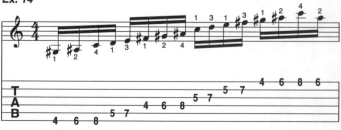

18

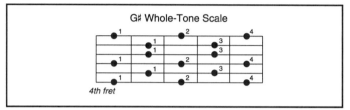

Diagram 14

G# Whole-Tone Scale

4th fret

These are but two of the many possible ways to play a whole-tone scale. Try playing it on one string, perhaps using three notes for every string. As always, make this scale and exercise your own by finding a place for it in your music.

Ex. 15 is an altered jazz scale, like Robbie mentioned. It is called a Super-Locrian or Jazz Melodic Minor Scale, up a half step from the root of a chord. Here we are presenting the G Super-Locrian (G altered scale). Notice it's exactly the same scale as A♭ jazz Melodic Minor Scale starting from the 7th scale degree, G.

Ex. 15

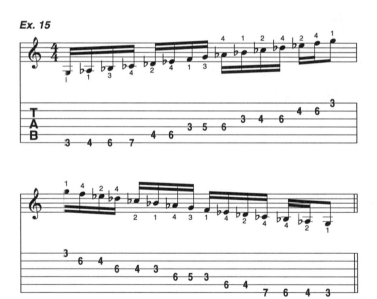

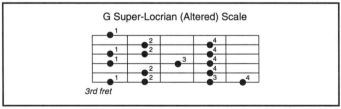

Diagram 15

G Super-Locrian (Altered) Scale

3rd fret

SCALE SEQUENCE EXERCISES
with MICHAEL WILTON

"Here is an example using a B major scale. Go up and back without a pause at the top. Start 1 note at a time, then 4's, then 3's. Remember to be legato, not staccato. Think of the mind and both hands as one."

NOTE:

1. Watch out for places where position transitions occur.

2. Remember these fingerings and the scale pattern are only suggestions; feel free to experiment.

3. Create your own sequence patterns. Practicing scales by using different sequences has been one of the most effective ways to reinforce your scale knowledge. It's not only a good test to see if you know the scale, but it also helps train your fingers and ears as well.

Ex. 16 is the B Major scale in two octaves as Michael plays it.

Ex. 16

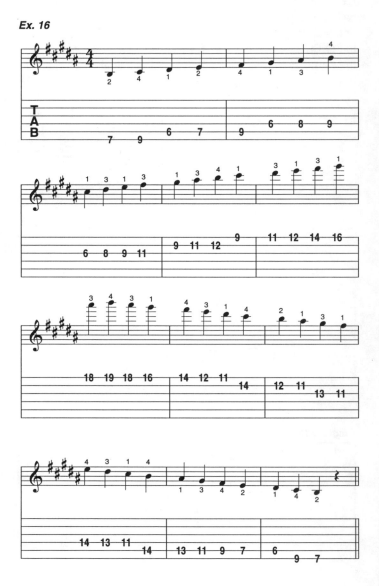

Diagram 16

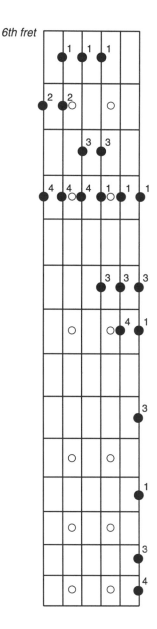

6th fret

Ex. 17 is the same scale played in a 4-group-note sequence.

Ex. 17

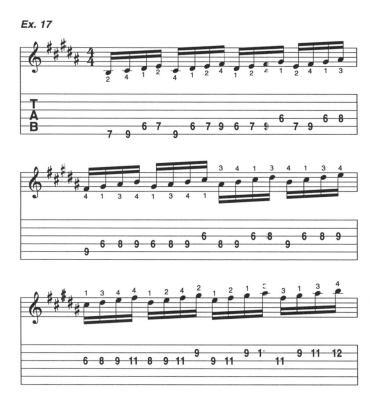

Ex. 18 is the same scale played in a 3-group-note sequence.

Ex. 18

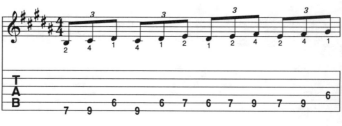

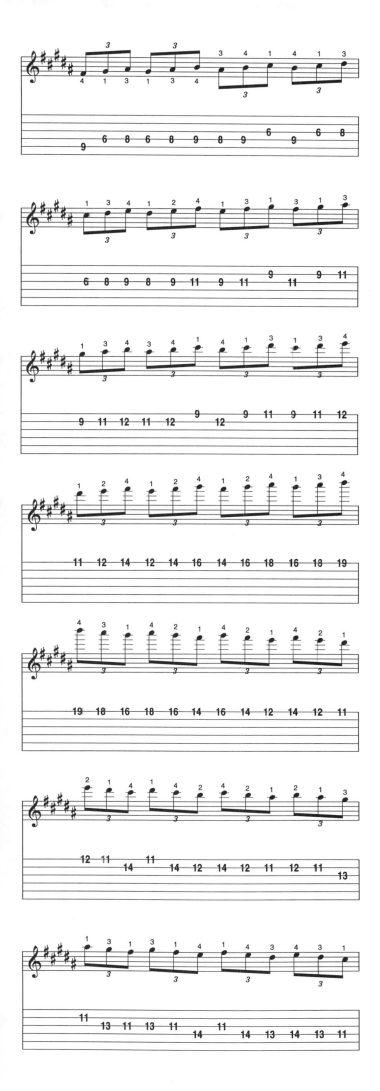

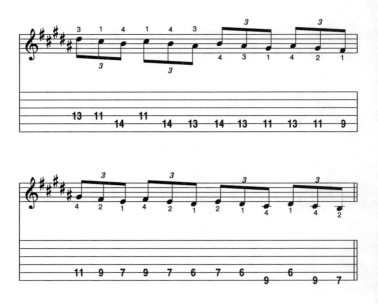

I like to work out with a 12-string before I go on-stage; play some barre chords and play some leads on 12-string. I like that a lot. It really toughens your hand up. When you go out and have a 6-string, you are ready for it. I just play blues and oldies, Beatles songs. Real bits and pieces of stuff.

—Joe Walsh

PUTTING IT ALL TOGETHER
with STEVE MORSE

"One thing to do while warming up is to literally get warm. Especially if you think about your future. Everybody needs to start thinking about that if they are going to spend a lifetime playing. Think about taking care of their muscles and tendons. The first step is to develop the good habit of washing your hands in warm water. This is to get your hands warmed up and of course to get them clean. Getting your hands literally warmed up makes it easier to stretch. Then start very slowly with the easiest exercise that seems to do any good. That's doing triplets. That's going 1, 2, 3, 1, 2, 3 across each string, using three fingers. I do different patterns on each position and move up a fret each time. I start on the low E string, F note and play F, F♯, G, then B♭, B, C on the A string and D♯, E, F on the D and so on, going up the strings and then back down. Stay in first position and then use fingers 2, 3 and 4 to play the same notes, starting on F♯ and going up and down the strings. Then move to the third position and use fingers 1, 3 and 4 to do major and minor scales with three notes per string, repeating a note on the G string that you will play on the B string, or playing a flat 5. It's almost a pentatonic pattern except three notes a string. You can play a minor or major pentatonic pattern three notes a string. I try to make it different each time I move up a fret, just so I don't do it too mindlessly. You have to think a little bit. The advantage of doing it this particular way is your pick changes direction every string. You get alternate picking exercise and you don't have to worry about starting in one direction, finishing the exercise, and then starting it again in the opposite direction. Every other time you've got a new direction. In the 4th position, I might do an E mixolydian pattern starting in 4th position starting on G♯,A, B, C♯,D, E F♯,G♯,A, B, C♯,D first finger on the B string E, F♯,G♯,G♯ again on the fourth position with your first finger A, B and the come back down. In 5th position I might do A diminished. A, B, C, D, D♯,F, F♯,G♯,A, B, C, D, D♯,F, F♯,G♯, A, B, slide it up one fret and then use the same scale coming down, starting with he fourth finger of the high E string with the C, B, and A, and come back down. The next one would be G♯ with the fourth finger. Go up and down the same scale. You can shift that last note and kind of add an extra note, rather then repeating the last note."

Ex. 19 is the chromatic 1, 2, 3 and 2, 3, 4 exercises, followed by G Natural Minor or Aeolian (or B♭ Major scale), followed by E Mixolydian (or A Major scale) and finished up with A Diminished scale, moving up one fret each time.

Ex. 19 — Chromatic with 1-2-3 Fingers

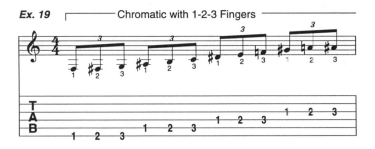

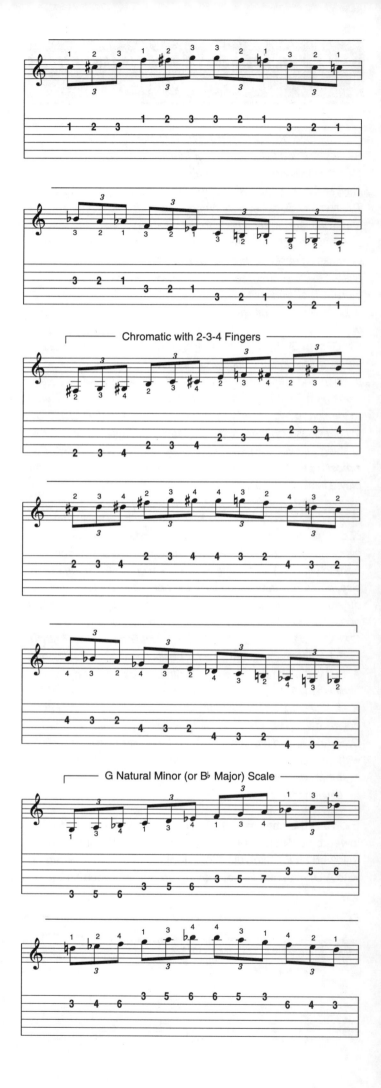

Chromatic with 2-3-4 Fingers

G Natural Minor (or B♭ Major) Scale

26

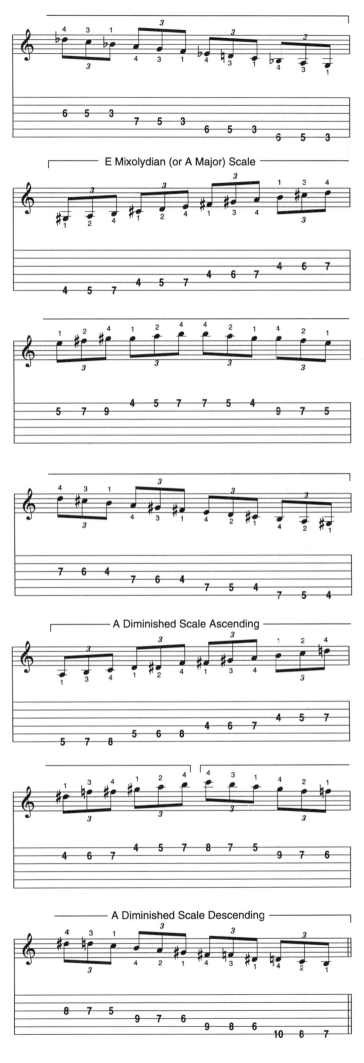

Diagram 19

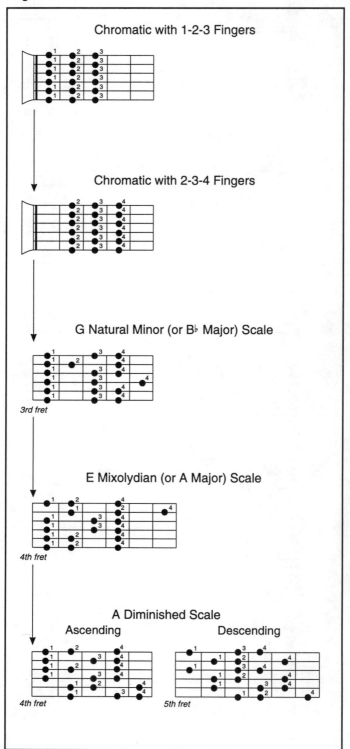

Chromatic with 1-2-3 Fingers

Chromatic with 2-3-4 Fingers

G Natural Minor (or B♭ Major) Scale

3rd fret

E Mixolydian (or A Major) Scale

4th fret

A Diminished Scale

Ascending

4th fret

Descending

5th fret

JAMMING SONGS AND MENTAL INFLUENCES
with RICHIE SAMBORA

"Scales were never anything to interest me as far as a warm-up exercise, before a gig or almost any other time. I tried to get into them, but they never hit me. I always had to play songs and wrench emotion out of them. That's the way I warmed up. I start getting deep for a half hour or so before I go on, and then can go out there and feel confident that I've got the instrument in my realm. But I don't play Bon Jovi songs to warm up; I leave the spontaneity for that on stage. I just jam and get into my own grooves. A lot of them are funk oriented, blues oriented, or just kind of out there. I'm by myself and I just start playing. Sometimes I get into different influences. If you want to practice your soaring bends you play David Gilmour stuff. 'Comfortably Numb' is a wonderful solo. If you want to practice your funk playing, you play Jimi Hendrix. You get into the tune and then you can get into your head, and play around with chord changes. A lot of times I just play the tune. Nobody is going to play like Jimi anyway. I don't really take licks per say. You just let it sink in and then you move it. On the Adventures of Ford Fairlane soundtrack album I did 'The Wind Cries Mary.' At the end of the song I tried to use as many Hendrix signature riffs as I could. I put them in that key and mess with them orchestrally, actually. If you want to practice your blues playing, you start playing Eric Clapton, Johnny Winter, B.B. King, or whatever you are going to go for. Get your vibrato cooking. As far as songs and changes go, anything off 'Layla' or by Cream. Then you get into Zeppelin, and you get rolling. Your mind goes off on its own and you become you. Sometimes, if I don't have enough time to warm up sufficiently, I use the Grip Master. That will get you close because it works all those muscles."

Note:

1. While Richie warms up by jamming, we decided to take some licks he may be playing and move them up the neck in the more traditional manner of warm-up exercises. This is a good way to practice a lick you want to nail down, while improving your hand coordination and ear training.

2. Continue these exercises in the same manner further up the neck and try other string combinations.

3. Similarly take any lick you are working on and move it up and down the neck repeatedly.

Ex. 20 is a lick taken and arranged from "Comfortably Numb," and moving up a half-step.

Ex. 20

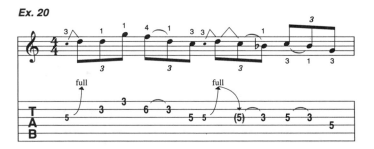

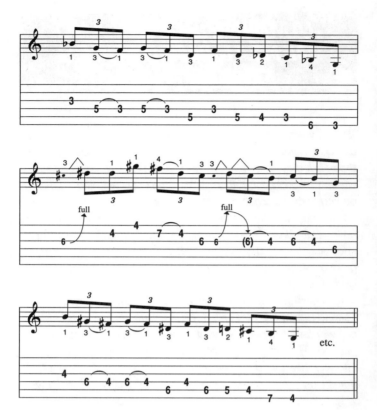

Ex. 21 is a lick from Clapton's version of "Hideaway," moving up in half steps.

Ex. 21

Ex. 22 is a lick from "Stairway to Heaven," moving up in half steps.

Ex. 22

BENDING IN TUNE AND VIBRATO

with NEAL SCHON

"I don't really have a warm-up exercise that I do. I would say a good warm-up exercise for me is being in tune with my stretches and vibrato. There are so many different types of vibrato. You can sit down with a piano, a tuning fork, or someone can hum out a note to you. Then, on the G string, play the note a whole step down from the note struck on the piano, and make sure that your stretching up is in tune with that note. Again, the piano player hits the note and you stretch up to the note and hit the vibrato. Use fast vibrato, use slow vibrato, use extremely slow vibrato, and make sure that note always comes back to the top when you come off it. Practice just holding the note forever while stretching up to it. I think that is a great warm-up exercise for all new guitar players that play a million notes. Practice just hitting one note and making it sing. Try stretching it up completely in tune with whatever kind of vibrato that you chose to put on it. And leave it there. Then go up to the B string and do the same thing. Go up to the E string and do the same thing. Then go back to the B string and go back to the G string and then stretch down on the G string. Pull it. Then move to the D. The D is more difficult, because they are wound strings. Try the A string, You can do it on all of them. I do that, trying to get my voice together on the guitar. It's so important to be able to bend in tune if you want it to sing like someone like Aretha Franklin or Stevie Wonder. You've got to do those types of things."

Ex. 23 is a vibrato exercise in fifth position with the third finger moving across the neck.

Note: 1. When adding vibrato to a note, relax your shoulder and wrist.
2. Fully sustain each note for a whole-note value
3. Concentrate on a stable and clear tone.
4. Try other places, other fingers, and different note values.
5. Experiment with different kinds of vibrato, such as short, wide, slow, rapid, etc.

Ex. 23

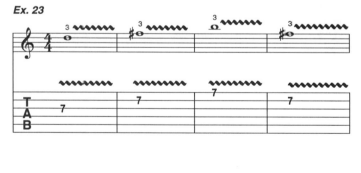

Ex. 24: Play an open E string (or Open A) and let it ring. Using the low E note (or A note) as your target, practice bending various notes on the E and B strings until they are perfectly in tune with the E or A note. Try this on other strings as well, and use Neal's suggestion to play fast, slow, or extremely slow vibrato on each note.

Ex. 24

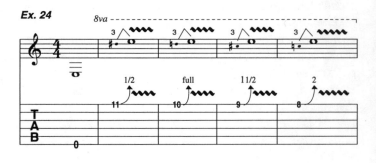

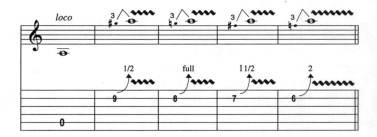

I don't like to sit down and practice for the sake of practicing. I warm up before shows, because I found that it's a necessity, and I do play better during the show.

—Slash

I've never sat down and practiced. To me, there is no better way to make it boring than to sit down and do the same thing over and over again for a long time. I'll never be Steve Vai because of that, but too bad. I just like to play and make music. I play with the stereo. That's recreation to me. I can put on AC/DC's 'Back in Black' and just solo over the whole record. That's a good workout.

—Scotti Hill (Skid Row)*